MIRACL
OF JESUS

Text by
Sue Hudson

Illustrations by
Graham Kennedy

Jesus Feeds a Large Crowd

Wherever Jesus went, crowds of people
gathered around Him.

One day, as Jesus was teaching a great
crowd, it became late in the day
and no one had eaten.

Jesus asked His followers to bring
to him any food they could find
amongst the crowd.

The disciples came back to Jesus
and brought with them a boy
who had five loaves of barley bread
and two little fish.

He offered them to Jesus.

Jesus told the people to sit down.

There were about 5,000 men plus women and children.

Then Jesus took the loaves of bread. He thanked God for the bread and then gave it to the people.

He did the same with the fish.

The people ate until they were full.

When they had finished, Jesus told the disciples to collect the leftovers in baskets. They filled twelve whole baskets. The people who saw this miracle were amazed and knew that Jesus was very special.

You can read this true story in John Chapter 6 Verses 1–15 in the New Testament part of the Bible

Jesus Calms a Storm

It was evening time.

Jesus had been speaking to crowds of
people all day and He was tired.
He said to his disciples,
'Come with me to the other side
of the lake.'

They got into the boat and set sail, leaving
the crowds on the lakeside.

Shortly after they set sail,
Jesus, who was sitting at the back
of the boat, fell asleep.

A very strong wind came up on the lake.
The waves began coming over the
sides and into the boat.

The disciples were very frightened.
They thought that they were
going to drown.

The disciples woke Jesus up.

He stood up and commanded the storm
'Quiet, be still!'

At once, the wind stopped and
the lake became calm.

Jesus asked His disciples, 'Why are you afraid? Do you still have no faith?'

The disciples were amazed and said to each other,

'What kind of man is this? Even the wind and the waves obey Him!'

You can read this true story in Mark Chapter 4 Verses 35–41 in the New Testament part of the Bible

Text © Visual Impact Resources Ltd 2004
Illustrations © Visual Impact Resources Ltd 2004

First Published 2004 by
Visual Impact Resources Ltd
7 Silverton Drive
Stenson Fields
Derby
DE24 3BU
ISBN 1-86024-504-8

3D Conversions by
Pinsharp 3D Graphics
Tel: 0151 494 2928

Design by
Ben Kennedy

Printed in the EU by
Print by Design Ltd
16 Castle Street, Bodmin
Cornwall
PL31 2DU
Tel: 0845 226 7306

Other 3D Bible stories available in this series include:

Parables of Jesus

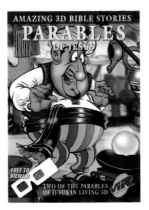

David & Goliath

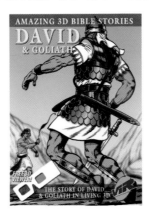

Jonah & the Big Fish

Published by
Visual Impact Resources Ltd
7 Silverton Drive
Stenson Fields
Derby
DE24 3BU

For more information about other 3D Bible products, visit
www.visual-impact-resources.co.uk